D0371523

CRUSH

If you're whistling while you work, leaving your house keys in the fridge, or seeing shooting stars in the afternoon, you've either got a **crush** — or need medical attention. Having a crush can make an ordinary day seem *extra*ordinary. It can make the sleepiest sleepyhead jump excitely out of bed and the laziest lump go for a jog after school.

It can also make you feel like crap.

That's because having a crush could mean *being* crushed. So, you ask, why bother? Why take that chance? Good question. Here's the less than useful answer: You can't help it. Human beings are wired that way. A crush isn't usually something you can wave away or avoid, like an annoying neighbor or pesky sibling. Crushes just happen, and they often happen out of the blue.

Maybe you're already a goner, having fallen for the foreign exchange student, coffeehouse clerk, box-office boy, or good friend. Or, perhaps you're on the lookout for someone fresh. (A new crush can be the best way to get over an old one, after all!) Whatever your status is, there's something for everyone—anyone with a heartbeat, that is—in *Crush*.

Learn fail-safe flirting techniques, cool comebacks, and how to plan dynamite dates. See how to handle heart-pounding moments and how to stare without looking like a stalker. Learn how to sustain new relationships and how to heal broken hearts.

When your crush first develops, you might feel dizzy, tongue-tied, or generally unwell, but soon you'll see the odds for love could very well fall in your favor. And that possibility makes a crush a gamble worth making.

TABLE OF CONTENTS

3. Hooking Him: How to Catch Your Crush 53

4. Crazy for Love: Overtaken by Obsession 69

7. Creep Alert: When Crushing Crosses the Line 109

8. Say It Isn't So: Bummer Endings, Happy Beginnings 119

You've Been Crushed: Sweaty Palms and Other Sure Signs

Lovesick Symptoms and Flare-Ups (From the Desk of Dr. Crush)

So what does it feel like to be crazy in love? That all depends on who you ask. As with most things, we all have our own way of dealing with this fabulous phenomenon. You might feel light-headed and woozy, or just plain sick. You might blush or break out—snap, crackle, or pop. You could feel anxious and aggravated, or warm and fuzzy. You could just stop eating. Or sleeping. Or thinking, breathing, *and* looking both ways when you cross the street. You will probably *start* doodling, daydreaming, picking out cuter outfits, and wearing shinier lip gloss.

One thing's for sure: Crushing is almost always complicated and sometimes even a little bit scary. With all these different lovesick symptoms, it can be hard to know whether you've come down with a bad cold or a bona fide crush. If you're not sure why you're acting so kooky, listen to your gut, talk to someone you trust, write in your journal, go for a walk, or simply stare at the clouds. Eventually, your big fat beating heart will tell you whether or not you've got a real, good, crazy case of crush.

PSST!
real-life quotes from real teens

HOW DO YOU KNOW?

❝ You know it's love when it's all you think or care about, and without it you're nothing, you cannot survive. It becomes a necessity in your life, to even see this person or watch him or her breathe or smile. You know it's love when it's pathetic. ❞ —15

Crushometer —Taking Your Love Temperature

So there's a new boy in school, and you think you might have a crush. But you might also just be a little bit bored and *wishing* for a crush. (It happens to the best of us.) Before you start passing notes or batting eyelids, consult the Crushometer to see where your emotions *really* stand.

PSST!

real-life quotes from real teens

YOU'VE GOT IT BAD WHEN ...

❝ ... you think about him constantly—and when you see him, you stare at him for a long time. You love spending time with him, and you remember every little thing he does or says. And no matter how much of an idiot he is, you can't stop thinking about him.**❞**—13

When you think about that new boy, you really just want to ...

squirm and squeal, fidget
and fuss, plot and plan,
... and touch his hair and
lick his face . . . . **scorchin' hot**

break out in song, ride
a unicorn, or make a collage ... **hot tamale**

share popcorn at the movies
and *maybe* even hold hands . . . . **hot potato**

catch a peek of him in his
gym shorts . . . . **warm and fuzzy**

poll your friends and see
what *they* think . . . . **lukewarm**

hook him up with your
neighbor or childhood chum . . **cool as a cucumber**

iron your socks . . . . **cold fish**

The Language of L-U-V

Ana behibak! (Arabic)

I love you! (English)

Je t'aime! / Je t'adore! (French)

Tá grá agam ort! (Gaelic)

Ich liebe dich! (German)

Aloha wau ia 'oe! (Hawaiian)

S' ayapo! (Greek)

Ani ohevet atah! (Hebrew)

Mein tumse pyar karta hoon! (Hindi)

Eg elska thig! (Icelandic)

Ti amo! (Italian)

Kimi o ai shiteru! (Japanese)

Qabang! (Klingon)

Tangsinul sarang ha yo! (Korean)

Ego te amo! (Latin)

Saya cintakan mu! (Malay)

Wo ai ni! (Chinese/Mandarin)

Muje se mu habbat hai! (Pakistani)

Tora dust midaram! (Persian/Farsi)

Iway ovelay ouyay! (Pig Latin)

Ja cie kocham! (Polish)

Eu te amo! (Portuguese)

Ya lyublyu tebya (Russian)

¡Te amo! / ¡Te quiero! (Spanish)

Nakupenda! (Swahili)

Jag älskar dig! (Swedish)

Mahal kita! (Tagalog/Filipino)

Chan rak khun! (Thai)

Seni seviyorum! (Turkish)

Em ye^u anh! (Vietnamese)

Rwy'n dy garu di! (Welsh)

Sweet, Sweet Baby: 10 Reasons a Crush Rocks

1. Flirting is fun! (Duh.)

2. A crush causes you to obsess about something other than stupid things that bug you (your science teacher's greasy mustache, your dad's Hawaiian shirt, or your little bro's smart-alecky comments).

3. It gives you an excuse to wear pretty sandals—even if it's raining.

4. It makes you want to paint your toes pink or dye your hair rich chocolate brown.

5. It forces you to strategize about the little things, like lunch spots, locker runs, and extracurricular activities.

6. It drives you to drink (water, lots of it) and pop pills (vitamins).

7. It helps you weed out fake friends—the ones who roll their eyes when you want to analyze that funny little noise he made when you crossed paths in the hall.

8. It makes the alarm clock seem less like an enemy and more like a friend.

9. It can make you smile, even when you're emptying the dishwasher or doing other similar tedious tasks.

10. There's always another—better—one, just around the corner ...

NO RHYME OR REASON

❝ When I have a crush, I smile all the time and feel good about myself when I'm near him. I feel safe around him. I'm still nervous about looking dumb to him, but he makes me feel safe, if that makes sense. ❞—14

Can You Relate? Crushes

Any of these sound familiar?

Celebrity: This is probably the most universal of all crushes. It usually involves *lots* of fantasies and elaborate daydreams. (Imagine a celebrity dream date picking you up in his helicopter, and later gushing thanks and love to you in his Oscar speech.)

Superhero: Who can resist a superhero? They save lives, act all mysterious, and wear cool costumes. This type of crush has roots in childhood and is often one's first crush after the babysitter or neighbor. Faves: Spider-Man, Batman, and Superman.

Class nerd: This means two things. The good news: You have a mind of your own and the ability to see beauty and charm in unexpected places. The bad news: Unless you keep it top secret, or believe you are cool enough for the both of you (if so, you go girl!), you're in for major mocking.

Former babysitter: He's older than you, but not too old. He used to let you stay up late watching TV, tucked you in, and said you were cute. Unfortunately … he's no longer paid to come over. So he no longer comes over.

Foreign exchange student: Someone new and exotic with an accent and a different way of looking at the world lands on your school lunch patio. What's not to like?

real-life quotes from real teens

CELEB CRUSH

❝I've had about one million crushes on celebrities and in real life about two. My all-time favorite is definitely Brad Pitt. What a sexy guy! Once me and a bunch, about 20, of girls were at a sleepover, and we decided to go around and reveal our secret crushes. No one volunteered to spill their secret, until I promised that I would reveal my secret crush. I had never admitted to having a crush on someone, so all the girls got excited and quickly gave up their guys' names. When it was finally my turn, I laughed and said, 'Brad Pitt!' It took a while for them to forgive me.❞—15

21

Nothing But Trouble: 10 Crushes to Steer Clear Of

1. **Your math teacher.** Math geeks can sometimes be cute, but it'll never work. He's too old and … he's also grading your next pop quiz.

2. **Your friend's brother.** If you value the friendship, it's not a wise plan. Your friend is sure to freak if she catches you kissing a sibling on family turf.

3. **The postman.** You'll never really know if he swings by on a regular basis to drop in on you, or just to drop off the mail. Not to mention the uniform.

4. **Your friend's uncle or dad.** Yuck! Enough said.

5. **The class clown or gossip.** Either way, too much potential exposure.

6. **The family dentist.** Fake toothache = real heartache. Besides, it makes the dental drool, spit, and bib even more humiliating than it already is.

7. **Most popular boy in school.** Who needs to be bothered with all that competition when his friend is just as cute?

8. **Your study buddy or lab partner.** At least not until you find a new brainiac who can also help you get straight As if your romance totally flops.

9. **Your best friend.** Unless you're absolutely *sure* he feels the same.

10. **Your friend's boyfriend.** This is a major *no-no* if you value any of your current friendships. You'll lose the friend in question (maybe several others, too), and the relationship probably won't last, either.

real-life quotes from real teens

MR. SOCIAL STUDIES

❝Jailbait, immoral, outrageous, call it what you may, but I had a definite crush on Mr. Social Studies. At first I thought I was crazy for loving Social Studies. Then I would find myself just dazing off, staring at his hands, or biting apprehensively at the tip of my pen. I realized I had quite the little crush on my hands. Yes, Mr. Social Studies was a bit older than me ... well a lot older. But I still wouldn't have minded some 'tutoring' on the side!

However, I must say, I must have a thing for teachers because now Mr. Gym isn't looking too bad at all.❞—16

Are You Ready for a Real-ationship?

Itching to take the next step with your sweetie? Take this handy quiz to find out how ready you *really* are to go from crush fantasy to relationship reality.

1. **You're working the register at the Dog on a Stick stand when you see your crush approaching the counter. You ...**

A. hyperventilate, drop to your knees, and use your elbows to crawl out the back.

B. head to your supervisor's office, surrender your uniform, and quit on the spot.

C. make eye contact and say, "Hey," but let your coworker take his order.

D. flash a big smile, offer him a free order of fries with his chili dog, and then finger feed them to him during your 15-minute break.

2. You and your neighbor have known each other since you were knee-high. One day, you spot him mowing the lawn with his shirt off and get that funny feeling in your stomach. You …

A. vow not to talk to him again until the first frost hits.

B. chug some pink stomach medicine and pray it was your mother's meatloaf that made you feel funny.

C. after careful thought, start hanging out with him to see how you *really* feel.

D. march over in your miniskirt, shut off the mower, and declare your love immediately.

3. Every time you try to catch your crush's gaze in the school hallway, he looks down and acts as if he's spellbound by his own shoes. You …

A. slowly die of embarrassment and spend the next few weeks wondering what's wrong with you.

B. start taking another route to class and find a new boy to fixate on.

C. try complimenting his taste in footwear. Maybe he's just shy?

D. drop your history book on his toe and demand to know why he's such a snob.

4. **You and your crush chatted and joked all through theater rehearsal. When you invite him to go over lines after hours, he drops the "I have a girl-friend" bomb. You ...**

A. stammer, stare blankly, and exit stage left.

B. start gathering your script together, while explaining that it was a purely work-related invite.

C. tell him how lucky his girlfriend is to have such a cool guy in her life.

D. give him a little wink and squeeze, and tell him his secret's safe with you.

5. **Your cute, new tutor has finally managed to make math make sense. But the only formula you want to memorize is: l + l = U 2 together 4ever. Problem is he's leaving for college in a few weeks. You ...**

A. think, *Why bother?* He's probably not interested anyway.

B. ask your parents to find you a new tutor. This is torture!

C. take a chance and tell him how you feel. Why not enjoy it while it lasts?!

D. trick him into kissing you by telling him it relaxes you before a test.

6. You've gone gaga for the gorgeous star of the latest cool flick. You have never felt this way about any boy you actually know, and think it might be love. You …

A. give up after-school activities and spend all your free time fantasizing about life with your superstar crush.

B. light candles and pray every night that he will magically fall in love with you.

C. see the movie four times *and* buy the DVD when it comes out, but keep your eyes open for a real potential boyfriend.

D. blow your life savings on a ticket to Hollywood and camp outside his house until he invites you in.

Answers:
Are You Ready for a Real-ationship?

If you answered all As:

You tend to be a little on the sensitive, shy side. You wear your heart on your sleeve, which can be a great quality, but you need to work on boosting your self-confidence before jumping into a relationship. Someday, in the not-so-distant future, you are going to make somebody feel very lucky in love!

If you answered all Bs:

You loathe confrontation. This makes you easy to get along with but hard to communicate with, which equals death in a relationship. Stop avoiding things that make you uncomfortable. It takes practice, so start with things that don't matter that much, like how your older brother always takes the big piece of cake. Once you improve your communication skills, you'll be ready for a relationship in no time.

If you answered all Cs:

You are a well-adjusted, balanced person. Of course, you're not perfect (who is?), but you understand the need to take chances when it comes to love. You still have some growing to do (who doesn't?), but when the right guy comes along, a beautiful romance is sure to bloom!

If you answered all Ds:

You have a definite flair for the dramatic. This makes you a lot of fun, and people are drawn to you. But sometimes you react a little too recklessly or assertively, and that can be a turnoff. Save the theatrics for the school play, and try toning it down (way down) when it comes to pursuing love. With a little coyness and a softer approach, you'll have boys beating down your dressing room door before the next curtain goes up.

On the Prowl:
Looking for Love

Hot Spots: 20 Places to Troll for a New Crush

When you imagine your potential new love, who do you see? A brooding intellectual? A lovable goofball? A handsome jock? Once you know what you're looking for, it's easier to figure out where to find him. But remember, the fewer restrictions you put on love, the more likely you are to find it!

To Find . . .	Head To . . .
the intellectual loner	the library or bookstore
a deep, dark dreamboat	the art-flick movie house
the six-pack sultan	the lifeguard stand
the dashing daredevil	the surf/snowboard shop
the sexy slacker	the skate park
the all-American sweetheart	the ice cream shop
the outdoorsy adventure man	the rock climbing gym
the strapping hunk	the gym or YMCA

To Find . . .	Head To . . .
a man who can move	hip-hop class
the lovable geek	the Apple Store
the typical techie	the video game section at Target
the hot nerd	chemistry class
the café rat	Starbucks
the mystery athlete from out of town	the visiting soccer/football/ water polo team
a geographically desirable guy	your older brother's room, where his best friends hang out
the well-prepared type	REI
the argumentative type	the debate team
the mature type	at the supermarket, helping Mom with the groceries
someone familiar	a friend's house or party
The One	wherever you least expect to find him ...

Poof! Whipping Up the Perfect Match

It's fun to daydream about your crush, even if you haven't actually met him yet. Putting your ideals (and i-don'ts) down on paper can help you clarify them—which can help bring you closer to actually *finding* who and what you're looking for. You might also learn something about yourself in the process. Sharpen your pencil, fill in the blanks on the next page, and set your dreams into motion.

ONE GIRL'S CRITERIA

❝He has to have good hygiene. He also has to be cute, strong (but not a stud—lots of muscles gross me out), not stupid but not a geek, and have some of the same interests as me. And he has to NOT come from a weird family.**❞**—13

♡	In My Dreams	In My Nightmares	In the Real World
Looks like:			
Acts like:			
Smells like:			
Treats me like:			
Thinks about:			
Ignores:			
Is really:			
Has:			
Loves:			
Likes:			
Loathes:			
Can:			
Won't ever:			
Will always:			

Cracking the Code: 3 Body Language Basics

Sometimes it's hard to tell if someone likes you or not, especially if one (or both!) of you is on the shy side. Body language can help you know if your crush thinks you're a total charmer—or a complete chump. Here's a starter list of surefire signals that you're NOT headed for heartbreak:

1. **"Eye" like you:** If he catches your eye and keeps it there for a little longer than usual, you may have just made a match! Another dead giveaway is if he watches your lips while you're talking. This kind of virtual lip-locking is a very good sign that he likes you—and might even secretly want to lay one on you.

2. **Hair-raising hints:** You may not know it yet, but your hair is a brilliant built-in flirting prop and a great way of gathering clues about how he really feels. Ever notice yourself toying with your locks when you're flirting as a way of being extra cute and coy? Boys do something similar: They sometimes run

their fingers through their hair as a way of saying, I'm cool, confident, and a great catch.

3. **You can say that again**: Mom always says: "It's not what you say, but how you say it." And when it comes to crushes, this couldn't be more true. Listen carefully to his voice and tone. Does he raise or lower his voice volume to match yours? Does he say "Hey" to you just a little differently than he says it to everyone else? Does he laugh at your jokes, even the bad ones? If so, things are sounding good!

THE LOOK OF LOVE LOST

❝I know it's over when he won't look at me. No matter how much I try to make eye contact with him, he goes out of his way to make sure I can't. And once I do, he gives me this guilty glance. Then I know it won't last much longer.❞—13

Astro-Logic

If you've been watching the universe for signs leading to love, you might want to use the stars to help guide the way. Here's a quick astrological briefing on your best romantic bets according to the zodiac.

If your sign is:

Aries (March 21-April 19)

Has the class flirt or comedian caught your eye? He might be the only one that can keep up with your fun and wild ways. That's because when it comes to love, you like to keep it lively. No couch potatoes or wallflowers for you!

Taurus (April 20-May 20)

You are a determined romantic who likes to be wooed and pampered by your partner. Your dream crush probably has style and talent. You might catch him scrawling lyrics or sketching a portrait of you in his notebook.

Gemini (May 21-June 21)

You are a free-spirited, fickle girl who refuses to settle. You might target the debate team captain one day and be bored by him the next. But no worries, someone completely different will knock your socks off again soon.

Cancer (June 22-July 22)

When it comes to relationships, you can be a bit on the moody side, but you always stay devoted to your mate. Home and family are very important to you, so look for someone who values those qualities, too.

Leo (July 23-August 22)

You like to be the center of attention but can be a very giving and romantic partner. Avoid hooking up with someone who wants to hog the spotlight or a catfight of king-sized proportions could ensue.

Virgo (August 23–September 22)

You are very grounded and willing to give as much or more to your partner as you receive. You might find yourself attracted to a party boy, but you're probably better off with a homebody.

Libra (September 23–October 23)

You love to be loved and are a true romantic. You tend to go for the pretty boys—the class flirt is probably on your list of lookers. Just be sure to seek out a sweetie with some substance beneath the charm.

Scorpio (October 24–November 21)

You are caring and extra passionate, but you're also willing to sting back twice as hard when stung. You need someone steady and solid who you can really get to know and trust on a deep level.

Sagittarius (November 22–December 21)

You are charming and inquisitive. You wonder about the world and are interested in many different types of people. This makes looking for love easy but zeroing in on it hard. You might find yourself happily surprised by romance with a former friend.

Capricorn (December 22-January 19)

You tend to be on the picky side and expect a lot from love. You might find yourself falling for the class pres, prom king, or captain of the debate team. You like a boy who knows what he wants and goes for it.

Aquarius (January 20-February 18)

You think finding love is fun, but you can be a little cautious about falling in it. You tend to go for spirited, intellectual types—like the kind of guy who actually *enjoys* science lab. You're also attracted to boys with a big heart, guys who really care about the world.

Pisces (February 19-March 20)

Your head may be in the clouds, but you're willing to come down to earth for true love. You're at your best when paired with someone who's willing to bare their soul and keep you grounded at the same time.

Hot or Not?

It has long been said that there's someone for everyone. You may think the new guy with the punk T-shirt and skinny legs is gorgeous, while your friend thinks his look is lame and his Mohawk is silly. What one friend finds annoying, another finds adorable. This is a good thing! It's confirmation that there are plenty of guys to go around. And that not every other girl on the planet has the hots for your man.

Unfortunately, it's not out of the realm of possibility that two friends might go for the same type, or even worse, the same *guy*. (Can you spell t-r-o-u-b-l-e?) If this happens to you, just remember that crushes come and go, but friends are forever. Sounds cheesy, but it's true.

To find out who you think is hot (or not!), take this quiz. Then, pass it on to your best buds to gauge how different (or alike) your tastes are.

	HOT	NOT
Winks hello		
Blushes when he sees you		
Surprises you with a balloon bouquet		
Writes epic poems about your toes		
Prefers boxers		
Has dimples		
Kisses with his eyes open		
Wears cologne		
Is the class clown		
Hangs out with your friends		
Is a drama geek		
Always lets you win		
Likes to thumb wrestle		

continued on page 44 . . .

	HOT	NOT
Calls you "dude"		
Dyes his hair blue		
Can recite the periodic table		
Sleeps till noon		
Has a goatee		
Sings in a band		
Is romantic at heart		
Has a hip sense of style		
Paints self-portraits		
Rides a Vespa		
Wants to be president		
Spends more time getting ready than you do		
Was prom king		
Loves his mother		
Likes you, and says so often		

HOT LISTED

❝My fantasy boyfriend: At the risk of sounding shallow, I'll start with looks. Blue eyes and brown hair. And tall. Very tall. Taller than me. I'm almost 5'10", so ideal height for my boyfriend would be about 6'4". Someone who will get along with my friends, and whose friends I can get along with. Someone who's VERY funny and knows how to make me smile. Someone I can talk to and trust and look into his eyes and know that everything is okay.❞—13

FAMILY AFFAIR

❝My ideal boyfriend would get along with my dad's side of the family. If my dad's side of the family disapproves, all is lost. But if my mother's side of the family disapproves, I can convince them he's not that bad.❞—13

The Heart of Feng Shui

Before you paint your room iceberg blue or adorn your bed with lots of frilly pillows, you might want to look to the East—to the Far East, that is. According to the ancient Chinese practice of feng shui (pronounced *fung shway*), even seemingly minor decorating decisions, like placing a scented candle or two on your nightstand, have an impact on whether you stay single or become part of a pair.

To put it simply, feng shui is about creating a personal space full of positive energy and harmony. It's about clearing clutter, conquering dust bunnies, and going with the *flow*. It's about blocking bad juju and arranging things in a particular, welcoming way. The energy in your home is called chi, and when you've got lots of chi flowing, life (and love!) is good.

So if you'd like to get in sync with your surroundings and call forth your crush, follow these feng shui tips and order up some l-u-v from the universe. With an open mind and some creative changes, it could be delivered to your doorstep in no time.

A Few Feng Shui Tips

1. Keep It Clean

A cluttered room = a cluttered heart. Don't store anything under your bed, empty your trash bin daily, and avoid using your floor as a laundry hamper. No cobwebs, mold, mildew, or dust allowed. Once you've done your spring clean, ring a bell or clap your hands (with gusto!) around the room to clear out all the old leftover energy.

2. Made in the Shade

Warm shades like pretty pinks, rich reds, chocolaty browns, and buttery yellows invite warm fuzzies into your life. Avoid cool colors, like light blues, greens, and grays.

3. One Is the Loneliest Number

Decorate the far right-hand corner of your room with pretty objects, in pairs if possible. Choose things like cute crystal hearts, fresh pink peonies, or red candles.

4. Keep a Lid on It

In feng shui, it is believed that good energy can escape through an exposed or open drain. So, if your room is near the bathroom, try to keep the toilet seat down—unless you're, um, using it—to prevent flushing any chances for romance down the drain! (This task may prove harder if you live with one or more members of the male species.)

5. Open-Door Policy

Boys may not actually be *allowed* into your bedroom, but it's still important to make sure your bedroom door opens easily and all the way. Doors that stick or squeak block romantic energy from flowing freely through your life. Make sure your doorknob is on nice and tight: A loose knob could mean you'll have a loose grip on love.

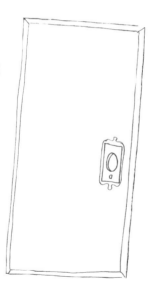

6. Bed-Vroom!

Place your bed opposite the door but not directly in front of it. Don't overdo it with lacy pillows, dolls, or stuffed animals. Bogging down your bed with these girly things suggests there's no room for boys in your world.

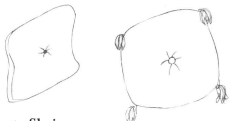

7. Your Time to Shrine

Construct a collage or shrine that symbolizes your perfect crush. Use symbolic images or items that celebrate the object of your affection, like photos, movie stubs, love doodles, or letters. Put your creation in a soothing, comfy spot where you're bound to see it every day. Think romantic thoughts when you meditate on it.

Crushes Mama Never Told You About

Here's what some real-life girls had to say about *their* unexpected crushes.

OLDER MAN

❝Of course I've had a crush on an older guy. They're more mature, bigger, stronger and just hotter in general. And they can drive.❞—15

BROTHER'S FRIEND

❝I liked him for about seven or eight years. He was my older brother's friend, Ryan. He was always really nice to me (not to be expected from my brother's friends) and yelled at his little brother when he made fun of me. I finally kissed him when I was in sixth or seventh grade, I think. He was really nice. I still talk to him sometimes.❞—14

PSST!
real-life quotes
from real teens

ANOTHER GIRL

❝ It was sort of a shock to me to realize I had a crush on a girl. I had been pretty sure I was straight, so I was really surprised and confused. I started to rethink everything about myself. That freaked me out—not the fact that I might not be straight, but the fact that I didn't know. It's really scary to feel like you don't know yourself anymore. I started to drive myself crazy. I kept trying to force myself to choose, boys or girls. After about a week of tearing my head apart, I realized that all of the gay/lesbian adults that I know well didn't come to realize that about themselves until their twenties, if not later. So I'm just playing it by ear, seeing what happens, no worry.**❞**—15

Hooking Him:
How to Catch
Your Crush

Get the Down Low on Your New Dream Boy

OK, Sherlock. You know you think he's adorable and that his smile makes you swoon. But how much do you *really* know about the object of your affection? The more you know about him—his hobbies, likes, dislikes, and character—the more you'll have to talk about when that "chance" meeting finally happens. You can ask him leading questions and get him to open up about things— like his job at water-ski camp last summer, annoying little brother, new skateboard, or favorite band. He's bound to be impressed by how enchanted and *enchanting*, interested and *interesting* you are. And if he turns out to be a total bore, you'll know that, too—before wasting time on someone who isn't really the guy you thought he was in the first place.

So, pull out your spy kit and get ready to do a little detective work. Everyone knows the key to being a good secret agent is the secret part. Don't be obvious and don't get caught, unless you *want* to look like a weirdo. Inquire nonchalantly to friends (his, yours, whosever), neighbors, and siblings. Observe his comings and goings, quirks and habits. Watch, listen, and learn. You'll be amazed by how much info you dig up!

PSST!
real-life quotes from real teens

TOO MUCH INFORMATION

❝When I have crushes I try to learn everything about them, kind of like being a stalker without having weird, nasty, violent, 'stalker-ish' feelings toward them. There was this one guy I liked for like four years, and now I'm close to his family because I spent so much time around them. I would make up really stupid reasons to call him, and then babble for like five minutes about absolutely nothing. My friend once called him and told him I loved him, and I called to clarify that I DIDN'T. It was really embarrassing. Another time, I invited his brother to a party because if his brother was there then he'd come. I ended up getting really mad at his brother and dumping my soda all over him. He ended up thinking it was really funny. I mean, come on—getting a drink dumped on your little brother. What more could a guy ask for?❞—15

Fail-Safe Methods of Flirting

Three times a charm

At least three separate verbal or non-verbal clues is about what it takes to get the "I'm starry-eyed for you" message across. The first time he's going to wonder if you are actually flirting or just being friendly. The second time, he'll start to get it, but he won't be prepared to respond in kind. The third time, he just might be ready to flirt right back at you.

Laugh a little

Show your dimples and giggle at his jokes. Touch his shoulder lightly and tell him how hilarious he is, especially if it's true.

Hang with your pack

Stay close to friends when you walk through a group of boys. Assign someone to report on who was checking out whom.

But also make yourself available

If you are out with friends, separate every so often. Otherwise, he'll never get the message.

If you *feel* cute, you *are* cute

Wear something you feel good in, and hold your head high. You'll look great.

Smile over your shoulder

Striking this asymmetrical pose is a serious sign that you're interested.

Give him the head-to-toe

A long, suggestive look is the surest crush signal you can send.

Trust that beating organ

Your heart does know best. Listen to it.

Tricks of the Trade

Perfect is boring, but that doesn't mean you shouldn't try to be your best, especially when you're cruising for a crush. The possibility that you might run smack-dab into your almost-sweetie exists every single time you leave the house. Unless you've actually inserted a tracking chip in his neck, you never know where or when the opportunity to beguile him might pop up. Isn't that scary ... and amazing?

Here are 10 tricks of the trade to help you be prepared for anything.

1. Carry lip gloss. Never leave home without it.

2. Have confidence. It's even better than lip gloss.

3. Smell great. Boys have sensitive noses.

4. Be coy and just a little bit mysterious.

5. Ask him for advice, but don't play dumb.

6. Laugh with him, but not *at* him — at least not at first.

7. Laugh at yourself. It shows that you have a sense of humor, and don't take yourself *too* seriously.

8. Be yourself. No one likes a fake.

9. Wear something that makes you *feel* as pretty as you *are*.

10. Want a lot out of life, and expect that you will get it.

THE WAITING GAME

❝I haven't really done anything too over the top to get noticed. I have stressed out over a guy though. I am more someone who waits for him to make the moves, which really tears me apart when he doesn't.❞ —13

Fancy Meeting You Here

Sometimes destiny needs a little shove. Obviously, you believe you and your crush were made for each other, but … if the universe has been too busy to throw you two together, you might have to step in and help it along. It's not meddling, it's masterminding. A "chance" meeting (or two) may be all you need to land your love.

There's an art to being in the right place at the right time, but there's also a science to it. You must take care to choose your planned run-ins thoughtfully. This requires skill, time, and attention. Think of yourself as a zoologist, studying the habitat of your favorite species, or as a sleek panther tracking her prey. Suss out his class schedule, lunch spot, weekend hangouts, practices, and where his mom drops him off in the a.m. Know where he's gonna be and when. Preparation and proximity make a perfect pair.

Concocting a logical—or at least semi-logical—reason for being where he also *happens* to be is likewise key. You don't want to look like a stalker—even if *technically* that's how you are sort of behaving. When you do finally "bump" into your crush, be coy and cool, sweet and subtle. He'll buy the act ... as long as you don't wind up *everywhere* he goes ...

THE FRESHMAN

❝My best friend and I had a crush on this older guy who went to the college near our middle school. We would ditch class to watch his car to see what time he had classes on what days. Eventually we knew his entire schedule. We left a note on his car, and we would ditch school to go over to the college and look for him. We never talked one-on-one, but he definitely knew who we were.❞—15

Smells Like Teen Spirit

If the odor of sweaty socks, skunk mist, and stinky cheese on a guy doesn't exactly inspire you to flirt, you're not alone. Your own icky odors can repel romance just as easily. But scent can also help set the mood and attract love. How you smell says a lot about you and can secretly influence your crush's frame of mind. The practice of aromatherapy goes back thousands of years. The legendary queen of Egypt, Cleopatra, was said to have used aroma-therapy to make perfumes, which helped her snare the likes of Julius Caesar and Marc Antony.

Luckily, you don't need to be royalty to smell like a princess. Just dab (not douse!) a bit of your favorite fragrance strate-gically behind your ears, underside of your wrists, or on the back of your knees, and you'll be like honey to his bee. Try gliding by your sweetie one sunny day, smelling sweet and luscious. Unless he's scentually impaired, he'll register your aroma. And next time you pass by (or go on your first date), he'll register it again. Pretty soon, that smell will have you deposited in his long-term memory bank.

Here's what to sniff around for, depending on what you want to say with your scent:

calling all casanovas . . . . . gardenia, patchouli, rose, sandalwood, strawberry, vanilla

pretty pick-me-ups . . . . . . bergamot, lemon verbena, grapefruit, peppermint, sweet orange, tangerine

let's chill . . . . coconut, cucumber melon, honeysuckle, lavender, myrrh

feeling cozy . . . . coco, coffee, musk, cinnamon, pine

exotic attraction . . . . jasmine, tuberose, orchid, passion flower, ylang ylang

The Hard to Get, Too Hard to Get Game

It's one of those stupid facts of life that many boys (not all, but lots) prefer it when a girl plays it cool, confident, and aloof. It's almost like they *want* you to give them the brush off (at least at first) so they can be the ones to chase and catch you. Pretty lame, right?

Don't sweat it. Make your crush think he is the hunter—even though the truth is you're the one wearing the bright orange vest and calling the shots. Like any sport, this type of hunting takes skill and practice. And there *is* such a thing as overkill. Study these examples to perfect your aim.

Hard to get: Give him an innocent hug—but nothing more—after your first date.

***Too* hard to get:** Blow him off completely with a "sorry someone better came along" text message before your first date.

Hard to get: Wait two days to return his call.

***Too* hard to get:** Wait two months to return his call.

Hard to get: When he asks you out, tell him you need to check your calendar first.

***Too* hard to get:** When he asks you out, tell him you need to check with your boyfriend first.

Hard to get: Casually mention that you don't need a relationship to be happy.

***Too* hard to get:** Casually mention that you don't want a relationship—EVER.

Hard to get: When he asks if he can kiss you goodnight, say, "I don't know … can you?" and flash an ever-so-subtle Mona Lisa smile.

***Too* hard to get:** When he asks if he can kiss you goodnight, stomp on his toe—just for the heck of it.

(Down)playing the Fool

We've all embarrassed ourselves from time to time.
Here are some cool comebacks to save you from those
mortifying moments.

Nightmare scenario: Class bully points out the HUGE
pimple on the tip of your nose to everyone within
shouting distance—including your crush.

Cool comeback: "My pimple will be gone in a few days,
but you'll have that face to deal with forever."

Nightmare scenario: Your crush asks you out for
Saturday night, and you let it slip that it's family bingo
night at your house. He raises a brow.

Cool comeback: "Yeah, so now you know my big secret:
I actually really LIKE bingo—and my family. How about
Friday night instead?"

Nightmare scenario: Your crush tells you that you have food on your face.

Cool comeback: "Oh, that. I'm saving it for later in case I get hungry during my afternoon sky-diving class."

A NOTEBOOK NIGHTMARE

❝The craziest thing I ever did was write a diary full of letters to a guy I liked in sixth grade. I would write about my life and how much I liked him, and then he found it because I was stupid and brought it to school. I thought I would die of embarrassment!❞—15

Crazy for Love: Overtaken by Obsession

Keeping It Cool (Avoiding the Pitfalls of Puppy Love)

When it comes to first (or second) love, it's nearly impossible not to get swept up, up, and away. But it's important to keep your head screwed on, even if your heart has let loose. Pace yourself. Let your relationship develop naturally and slowly. If your love takes off too soon, you could be in for a crash landing.

You might be thinking, *I'm over the moon! How am I supposed to come down to earth?* It's not easy, but it IS possible. How? Don't start shopping for next year's Valentine's Day gift just yet or plotting how you'll both get into the same college. Stay in the moment—and *enjoy* it. Maintain balance in your life—don't dump your friends just because you're head over heels. Keep up your studies, hobbies, and family life. Stay interested in life outside the love part. It'll make you more interesting.

No boy wants a desperate, clingy girl without a universe of her own. And if he does, there's a little something wrong with him, too.

MAD ABOUT YOU

❝ I was in love with this guy I met in the summer. He was everything I always wanted in a guy. EVERYTHING. We had the greatest time together, and I'd never been happier. But then summer ended, and I haven't talked to him since. For about two months after, I was so depressed because I had no idea how there could be someone else out there like him. I have a picture of him that I looked at everyday, but when I did that I would miss him more. So I had my bro hide it. Yeah, I know it sounds weird, but that's the only way I could deal. There is a chance I will see him next summer though, which will make me *so* happy.**❞**—15

You Know You're Obsessed When

♡ you can't remember what sign you are, but read your crush's horoscope every day.

♡ you consult your Magic 8-Ball every five minutes about whether he *likes* you likes you, or not.

♡ you've already picked out your wedding dress—and your children's names.

♡ you'd sacrifice your brother, sister, or pet to be with him.

♡ you've filled an entire notebook with heart doodles and Mrs. [*insert you-know-who's last name here*].

♡ you wake up, go to sleep, and spend the entire day thinking about him.

♡ you think it might be a good idea to use your college savings to buy him a car so he'll *have* to offer you a lift to school in the morning.

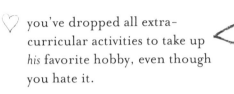 you've dropped all extra-curricular activities to take up *his* favorite hobby, even though you hate it.

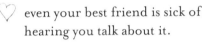 even your best friend is sick of hearing you talk about it.

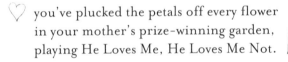 you've plucked the petals off every flower in your mother's prize-winning garden, playing He Loves Me, He Loves Me Not.

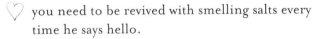 you need to be revived with smelling salts every time he says hello.

you can't even imagine falling for anybody else—ever.

How to Curb That Crazy Behavior

By now you probably realize that you have, indeed, become a bit obsessed. Here are some pointers to help you get control of your actions and direct that kooky energy into a more practical direction.

Symptom: You've just been fitted with a corrective brace for repetitive stress injury, brought on by writing his name in your notebook over and over (and over) again.

Remedy: Find a more constructive way to express your love—like writing a poem, doing a painting, climbing a mountain, or planting a tree in his honor.

Symptom: There's an impression of a phone receiver on your face from repeatedly calling him and hanging up every time he says "Hello?" in that oh-so-adorable voice.

Remedy: Take a chance and stay on the line! What have you got to lose? If he isn't receptive, you'll know it's time to find a new (more promising) object of desire.

Symptom: His neighbors have started to wave and smile as you walk past his house (again).

Remedy: Take up a new hobby or volunteer at the local soup kitchen—you've got too much time on your hands! Think of ways to work on yourself. Remember, again, that a better you is a more desirable you.

A VISION

❝ During my first art class, we created sculptures with brown, glossy clay. The class was silent as I looked up and noticed a pair of soft, blue eyes staring at me. I spotted a smile on his freckled face. It was one of those smiles that you don't see every day. The beat of my heart was like a racehorse running for first. I could see stars twirling above my head and red hearts popping out. My constant day-dreaming caused me to fall behind on my sculpture. The rest of the day, I fantasized. I had the symptoms of 'love,' according to my friend Sammy. It took three days to find out the name of the boy I had a crush on. I wrote his name all over my notebooks and on little notes kept sacred in my bedroom desk drawer. ❞ —14

Which Is Worse?

Watching your crush flirt with your bff **or** supergluing your lips to your locker?

Splitting your pants in front of your crush **or** eating a slug?

Being stood-up by your crush **or** never having been asked out by him in the first place?

Having your ex trash-talk you to your crush **or** being shipped off to boarding school in Siberia?

Bumping into your crush while walking your neighbor's giant shaved poodle **or** getting a bad haircut?

Having the school gossip tell your crush how you feel in front of five of his friends ***or*** him never knowing you even exist?

Seeing your crush kiss his new girlfriend *OR* flunking PE?

Accidentally letting out a **or** big smelly belch in front of your crush shaving off your eyebrows?

Getting caught doodling "I ♡ [*insert crush's name here*]" **or** wearing two different shoes to school all day?

Never getting over your first crush *or* never even having one?

In the Name of Love, Stop: 10 Ways to Not Embarrass Yourself

If you've gone seriously loco for love, listen up: Some things really *are* better left unsaid. If you haven't already embarrassed yourself by proclaiming your love in a public and inappropriate fashion, be thankful. If you *have* already embarrassed yourself, don't worry—it could have been worse. Besides, somebody else is bound to make an even bigger fool of her/himself soon, and by that time, your crazy crush behavior will just be a fading memory.

Either way, read this list. Then read it again. Consider it a gift from the love gods and do your best to adhere to its contents.

Do not:

1. doodle "[*insert his name here*] loves [*insert your name here*]" in permanent ink all over his locker, bike, or car.

2. reprogram his iPod entirely with classic cheesy love songs, including the one you wrote for him.

3. write an epic poem about your love and recite it to him in English class.

4. show up at his house every morning and follow him to school, walking just 12 short paces behind.

5. send him e-cards for his parents' anniversary, Valentine's Day, Christmas, the World Series, the World Cup, his dog's birthday … and for absolutely no reason at all.

6. tell all his friends not to worry—they'll definitely be invited to the wedding.

7. beg, bribe, or blackmail him into dating you.

8. ask his dad or little brother to put in a good word for you.

9. suggest wearing matching outfits to school.

10. buy him a leash or permanently attach yourself to his hip.

You Got Him.
So, Now What?

Love Is in the Air

You did it. You scored your crush. Do you have any idea what kind of coup this is?

But, wait. Just because finding love is so hard, doesn't mean keeping it is going to be easy. Even though it seems totally unfair, having a relationship can be just as hard—or harder—than finding one. Think about how many couples split up. OK, now *stop* thinking about it.

But do keep thinking about what a great thing love is—and how lucky you are to be starting something so cool with your crush. Who knows how things will go? Things could get serious … or you could get seriously bored. (Stranger things have happened.)

For now, just take things slowly, day by day. Enjoy things as they unfold. Appreciate each moment. You are sure to have more of them—whether with this beau or an entirely new one down the line.

Cuddle Flicks: 15 Movies to Set the Mood

1. *She's the Man* (2006)

2. *Along Came Polly* (2004)

3. *Win a Date With Tad Hamilton* (2004)

4. *13 Going on 30* (2004)

5. *Sweet Home Alabama* (2002)

6. *A Knight's Tale* (2001)

7. *Serendipity* (2001)

8. *Never Been Kissed* (1999)

9. *Notting Hill* (1999)

10. *10 Things I Hate About You* (1999)

11. *Shakespeare in Love* (1998)

12. *Clueless* (1995)

13. *Say Anything* (1989)

14. *The Princess Bride* (1987)

15. *Sixteen Candles* (1984)

Smack Attack

OK, now you're a couple. That means you're probably going to be kissing. Of course, when it comes to smooching, there's no teacher quite like personal experience. But here are a few tips to help you master your mouth—and his.

- **Breath check.** Make sure you've brushed and flossed recently, if possible. If not, pop a mint. It's not called "death breath" for nothing.

- **Make yourself comfy.** Kissing is awkward enough without having to act like you're perfectly comfortable balancing on your tiptoes.

- **Go easy, Tiger.** You don't want to break your nose, bite his lip, or chip a tooth.

- **Shut your lids, at least at first.** It's less embarrassing that way. And that way you can imagine you're in a field of poppies or at the beach with the surf crashing behind you, instead of in the school parking lot.

- **Start with your lips closed.** No tongue jamming! It's gross. Tongue action should be taken slowly, when the kiss progresses.

- **Wet your whistle.** A dry mouth is not very kissable — just don't drool or anything. Try gently licking his lips to lube 'em up, if need be.

- **Take it slow with the tongue.** Imagine you're an explorer on a leisurely expedition — not lost at sea stuck in a typhoon. Move your tongue around the mouth, teeth, tongue, and lips. Tongue to tongue can be nice, too.

- **Nip it in the bud.** A very soft little love bite on the lip is nice. If you'd like to see him again, no chomping!

- **Breathe.** In through your nose. Out through your nose. In through your nose. Out through your nose.

- **Eskimo kiss.** Rub noses, arms, cheeks, feet.

- **Practice makes perfect!**

TNT: 10 Dynamite Dates

As if landing your crush wasn't tough enough, now you have to worry about keeping him. You can't exactly control whether or not your spark sputters, but you can try to keep it glowing by planning fun and flirty ways to spend time together.

Here are a few suggestions:

1. Surprise him with a gourmet picnic (complete with sparkling cider and fresh green grapes to feed him!).

2. Hunt down front-row tickets to his favorite band.

3. Act like little kids and head to the park at sunset. Hit the seesaw and swings while holding hands.

4. Buy a giant pack of bubble gum and blow bubbles into each other's mouths.

5. Take a ride in a blimp, helicopter, or hot-air balloon.

6. Go for sushi or some other exotic cuisine.

7. Ride bikes down to the creek, river or lake, and sit on the bank and talk until the fireflies come out.

8. Rent his favorite video and order Chinese takeout. Read your fortunes out loud to each other.

9. Share a giant milkshake at the local diner.

10. Go to the zoo to see the baby pandas (or lions or tigers or bears, oh my!).

Getting Cozy: 20 Songs to Snuggle To

1. "Honey and the Moon"–Joseph Arthur

2. "I'm in Love"–Audio Bullys

3. "Beautiful"–James Blunt

4. "I Miss You"–Blink 182

5. "Wonderful Love"–Creeper Lagoon

6. "Thank You"–Dido

7. "Northern Sky"–Nick Drake

8. "Secret Heart"–Feist (or Ron Sexsmith)

9. "In Your Eyes"–Peter Gabriel

10. "The Birds Will Sing for Us"–Ed Harcourt

11. "Such Great Heights"–Iron & Wine
    (or The Postal Service)

12. "Maybe I'm Amazed"–Jem (or Paul McCartney)

13. "Somewhere Only We Know"—Keane

14. "Time After Time"—Cyndi Lauper

15. "Let My Love Open the Door"—M. Ward

16. "Cartwheels"—The Reindeer Section

17. "By Your Side"—Sade

18. "Dia de Enero"—Shakira

19. "You're the Best Thing"—The Style Council

20. "In the Cold, Cold Night"—The White Stripes

She's Crafty

Anybody can walk into a store and find a cool gift to buy. But if you want to show your new beau that his girl (that's you!) is far from ordinary, get crafty: Make him something special with your very own loving hands.

Little handcrafted mementos are even sweeter as spontaneous "there's no good reason except I like you" gifts.

He'll be surprised, flattered, and touched by your gesture. Take some time to really *think* about your crush before you get crackin'. Let his personality, hobbies, and likes inspire you to create something for him that is extraordinary, just like you.

Is he the literary type?

Sign up for a bookbinding or papermaking class, and craft him a handsome handbound blank book in which he can write his innermost thoughts.

Got a music geek in your life?

Put together an amazing playlist of his favorite tunes, complete with a set of lyrics to accompany each song.

Your bf like to snowboard?

Knit him some colorful winter socks (with individual toes!) or a nice long scarf to match his gear.

Does your sweetie have a sweet tooth?

Bake and carefully decorate a basket of heart-shaped cookies. Use frosting to spell out cute messages, or go gourmet by adding swirled chunks of shaved Belgian chocolate.

Love Busters: 20 Dating Don'ts

Sometimes it's hard to figure out how much is too much—or too little—when it comes to love. Even the most solid relationship needs to be handled with care. When you're part of a pair, you can't always just say or do what you want, whenever you want. You have to consider how the other person might react. No matter how well your boyfriend plays down his sensitive side, he's probably a big ol' softie on the inside, just like you. Unless you're really not that into him, there are *some* behaviors you should definitely avoid.

Do not:

1. baby talk to him in front of his friends.

2. laugh when he tries to kiss you …

3. or roll your eyes at his jokes.

4. tell him you only want to talk about *you*.

5. stop brushing and showering.

6. dress like a nun.

7. flirt with his friends.

8. call him by your ex's name, especially more than once.

9. wipe your mouth off after he kisses you hello.

10. eat a clove of garlic before every date.

11. refuse to acknowledge him in public.

12. barf in his lap.

13. roll your eyes when he tells you how much he likes you.

14. get caught snooping.

15. drill him about his ex.

16. give him a karate chop every time he says something you don't like.

17. drool.

18. belch the words: "I want to date other people."

19. scarf down your lunch—and his—without swallowing.

20. check his call log and dial every number you don't recognize to see if it's a girl.

Trouble on the Horizon

Just because there's a leak in your boat, that doesn't mean your relationship is a total sinker. Unless he's already cruising somebody else, you're still afloat. Don't panic, but do slip on some water wings, patch up those holes, and toss your sweetie a lifejacket. Here's how:

◐ Wishing it away never works. Talk to (but not at) your boyfriend about what's up with your relationship—find out what he really thinks. Once you both open up, you'll probably feel tighter and closer.

◑ Think back to the way things were in the beginning. Did you spend more—or less—time together? Did you laugh harder at his jokes? Did you look at him differently? Try to recapture some of that early magic.

◒ Plan a fun date night, just the two of you—no friends, no texting, no cells.

◓ Pay attention to your partner. This doesn't mean staring at him like you're out to win a contest or watching him like an eBay bid in the final few seconds of a purchase. But do try to shut your trap long enough to let him talk. You might be surprised by how much he has to say when you give him the chance.

G Learn to like (or at least appreciate some aspect of) his favorite hobby. You don't have to know how to skate to learn what an ollie is—and to see that it takes serious skill. And you don't have to paint your face or wear a giant foam finger to enjoy an afternoon football game together.

G Humdrum makes things glum. Mix it up and try something new. Go for Thai food instead of hitting the same old pizza place. Plan a romantic picnic in your living room, or take a rock climbing class together. Just do *something*—any-thing—out of the ordinary.

Surprise him by slipping a playful note in his math book or writing him a flirtatious text message. It'll remind him how cute and coy his girl can be ...

Don't ask him what's wrong every five minutes, and don't accuse him of wanting to be someplace—or with someone—else.

Spend time on yourself. Pick up those old knitting needles that have almost fossilized in your closet or that soccer ball you've dropped. A better you leads to a better relationship.

Know when to bail out if need be. Sometimes, it's better to go it alone and swim for dry land than stay with a ship that's wrecked beyond repair.

Completely Crushed: Unrequited Love

The Utter Agony of Being Dissed

Without a doubt, suffering unrequited love—love that is not, has not, and never will be returned—is PURE torture. Lots of people would rather be dumped cold than simply left out in it, without even the chance to have experienced romance with the object of their affection. At least if you've been dumped, you *had* a relationship, however short-lived or lame it was.

It might comfort you to know that you're not alone in your agony. Unrequited love is probably the most classic of all afflictions. It has inspired great literature, art, and music for ages. One of the most tragic and famous examples is from all the way back in the 13th century. The Italian poet Dante Alighieri fell for his crush Beatrice at first sight, when he was just nine years old! He never really knew her, beyond exchanging occasional greetings in the street, but devoted much of his life (and work) to loving her. Ugh. And remember how poor Charlie Brown from *The Peanuts* pined away for the unattainable Little Red-Haired Girl?

Like he once said, "Nothing takes the taste out of peanut butter quite like unrequited love."

Some people say the best way to get over unrequited love is to find a new crush. Close friends and hot chocolate can also help. But, unfortunately, time—lots of it—is the biggest healer.

PSST!
real-life quotes from real teens

END OF DISS-CUSSION

❝He was the perfect guy, and we became *really* good friends over the summer. I knew he wasn't my boyfriend, but it still hurt really bad when I found out he got a girlfriend because he had told me he didn't want to 'rush into anything.'❞—13

Warning Signs: 10 Ways to Tell He's Not Really Into You

Sometimes (OK, lots of times), it's hard to accept the obvious—especially when it's the exact opposite of what you so desperately want to be true. Sometimes, the truth sucks. And sometimes, even your friends won't point out what seems pretty clear, if they know it's going to hurt you. And so, *sometimes*, you have to suck it up and face reality, all by yourself.

The clues listed below tell you that his heart is most likely elsewhere. Once you've read 'em, recognized 'em, and wept, you should try to move on to something—or someone—more promising.

1. He can't seem to remember your name, even though you've been introduced more than once.

2. He seems distracted or looks off into the distance when you talk.

3. He calls you homeboy, chief, or bro.

4. You're always the one to call, email, text, IM, and say "hi." And he doesn't always respond.

5. He asks for your advice about other girls.

6. He never touches you, even just playfully on the arm or leg or whatever.

7. He gets up and walks away when you sit next to him at lunch.

8. He rarely, if ever, suggests hanging out—and when *you* do, he usually says no.

9. He ignores you in front of his friends.

10. The first three digits of the home phone number he gave you are 555. The second four spell out something gross.

Letting Him Know, Anyway

So, you've had this secret crush for like a year. And you are pretty sure he's not into you. Do you go ahead and tell him anyway?

Spilling the beans can be a risky move, especially if you feel like it could do damage to your friendship or risk your too-cool-for-school rep. Sometimes, if you're really sure he's not wanting to be your homecoming king, it's better to just let sleeping dogs lie. (The dog!)

However, it *could* also make you feel better to get it off your chest. For some, it's the only way to really move on. If you choose to go that route, there is, unfortunately, no perfect "I really like you a lot even though I'm pretty sure you don't like me" script to Google and rehearse. So, take some time to figure out what (if anything) you really want to say, the reason you are saying it, and how you want it to come out. Just remember that although it may be you in the loves-me-not corner this round, he might have been there in the last. Meaning: He'll probably understand,

and might even appreciate, your honesty. He may even surprise you with something unexpected. But don't go in expecting that.

The bottom line is that, after you 'fess up, you'll finally know how *he* feels, for sure. And however things turn out, in the end ... you'll be just fine.

PSST!

real-life quotes from real teens

RISKY DISCLOSURES

❝I write guys notes sometimes, just random things, and, if I like them enough, I put my cell phone number in the note. Have I ever gotten caught? Well, because I am so out there and obvious, I am catching myself before he can catch me. It comes out as part of my personality and that way he can't tell that I am crushing on him.**❞**–16

Fantasy Penalties for Lame, Unrequited Crushes

THE CRIME	THE PENALTY
The Story Repeater	Tongue lopped off and fed to stray dogs.
The Bragger	All his friends laugh and point each time he walks into the room. No explanation given—ever.
The Interrupter	Bird poops on head each time he cuts anyone off mid-sentence (even when indoors).
The Whiner	Frog literally gets stuck in throat.

The Chronically Late . .	Sleeps through final exams and has to repeat entire year.
The Neglectful Borrower	New pants tear each time he bends over until 21st birthday.
The Kiss Up	Permanently loses ability to blink. Teeth fall out.
The Part-Time Lover . .	Falls in love with the wrong girl who cheats on him incessantly.
The Social Climber . . .	Forced to take job handing out flyers on busy street corner while dressed as chicken.
The Table Tapper	Loses thumbs in freak boating accident. Hair grows on palms.

Creep Alert: When Crushing Crosses the Line

Dear Loser Letter

Maybe your crush turned into a boyfriend. Maybe he broke your heart. Or maybe, just maybe, he turned out to be a loser. If you're not sure, here are some tell-tale signs:

Does he follow you around like a little lost lapdog and call, text, and email you constantly? Does he simply refuse to catch a clue, even though you've been clear about your lack of feelings?

If his wooing ways are starting to seem more freakish than flattering, then a "see ya wouldn't wanna be ya" letter may be just what you need to sever ties.

See the list on pages 112 and 113 to fill in the blanks.

Dear [*fill in name or other choice word here*],

I don't know if you've heard this before, but you're start-ing to make me want to [*choose from list A*]. **I've tried to tell you I'd like to** [*choose from list B*], **but you don't seem to listen. I think you should focus on** [*choose from list C*] **instead of me. I know we had some really** [*choose from list D*] **times, but I see you more like a** [*choose from list E*]. **I'm sure you'll have better luck** [*choose from list F*]. **I want you to know that I'll always be** [*choose from list G*]. **So take care and please** [*choose from list H*]!

So long for good this time,

[*Fill in your name here*]

a

peel off my own skin
transfer schools
swear off dating for good

b

only be friends
pretend we never met
run when I see you

c

another girl
the priesthood
your rock collection

d

OK
"swell"
forgetful

e

nuisance
good friend
distant relative

F

with your next relationship
in Vegas
if you keep your fingers crossed

G

a little scared by you
the one you wouldn't leave alone
sorry I didn't realize all this sooner

H

take me off speed dial
give me a call when you're in love with someone else
stop spying on me

PSST!
real-life quotes
from real teens

THE BRUSH-OFF

❝ Frankly, the way I've always 'dropped hints' that
I don't like someone is this: I avoid all possible
confrontation. Hey, don't knock it until you try it.
It's surprisingly effective.❞ —16

Total Sweetheart or Psycho Stalker?

If you're wondering if your new boy might be taking the crazy-for-you thing a little (or a lot) too far, he probably is. But sometimes, when it comes to crushing, it can be hard to tell. Check out the chart below to sort out the sweethearts from the stalkers.

Your new crush ...	Sweetheart	Stalker
calls you every day	χ	
calls you every hour		χ
had your name tattooed on his forehead		χ
always seems happy to see you	χ	
hired a PI to spy on you when you're not together		χ
likes to hold hands in public	χ	
is nice to your mom	χ	
has started camping outside your house		χ

	Sweetheart	Stalker
shows up uninvited to family BBQs, girls' nights, and doctor's appointments		X
sends you cute texts once a day	X	
follows you into the bathroom twice a day		X
constantly pumps your friends for dirt on you, even though you've asked him not to		X
surprises you with a big bouquet of flowers on your birthday	X	
shaves your initials into the back of his head		X
tells you how cute you look	X	
wants you two to dress like twins		X
doesn't want you to talk to other boys—not even your brother		X
carries your backpack	X	
isn't kidding when he slings you over his shoulder and calls you "my woman"		X

Creepy Crush Comebacks

Got an unwelcome admirer hassling you with come-ons? Here are a few clever comebacks to keep in mind when he strikes ... again:

Creep: What's shakin', baby?
You: Your double chin.

Creep: Hey, honey, what's your sign?
You: Stop.

Creep: Nice butt.
You: Thanks, same to you. Oh, sorry, that's your face!

Creep: I know you want me.
You: Yeah, I want you to leave me alone.

Creep: I can make your wildest dreams come true.
You: Really? Because this feels like a nightmare.

Fright Show: 15 Scary Crush Movies

1. *Wicker Park* (2004)
2. *My Date With Drew* (2002)
3. *SwimFan* (2002)
4. *He Loves Me, He Loves Me Not* (2001)
5. *Cruel Intentions* (1999)
6. *What Lies Beneath* (1999)
7. *The Cable Guy* (1996)
8. *Fear* (1996)
9. *The Crush* (1993)
10. *Single White Female* (1992)
11. *Misery* (1990)
12. *Fatal Attraction* (1986)
13. *Play Misty for Me* (1971)
14. *Rebecca* (1940)
15. *Gaslight* (1944)

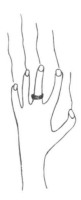

Say It Isn't So:
Bummer Endings,
Happy Beginnings

So Long, Farewell, Auf Wiedersehen

Move on. Let it be. Put the past behind you.

It's all so easy to say but so hard to do. Why? Well, that's complicated. It might simply be that your hopes have been dashed or that you lost the person you felt closest to. It could be that you've been hurt, humiliated, and betrayed. Or just that things simply didn't go the way you wanted.

Letting go of love, or the hope for it in a particular person, can be tough—no matter the circumstances. But there *are* things you can do to ease the pain. Unfortunately, you can't get over someone on cue. So exactly how much time *will* you need? That all depends on certain factors: Primarily, how long you were together (were you ever together?) and how it ended. It also depends on you. There's no mathematical formula, no magic ending bell. Everybody deals with things in their own time. Kind of a relief *and* a drag, isn't it?

PSST!

real-life quotes from real teens

PARTING IS SUCH SWEET SORROW

❝There was this guy I met last summer, and he is two years older than me. We both had the greatest time and talked about everything (we were both counselors at camp). There were times where we got super close, but nothing happened. I was so happy for those three weeks. But camp ended, and we haven't talked since. I have a bunch of friends who go to school with him, and they tell me how he has a bad rep with girls. But I saw him a different way and knew he wasn't like that.❞—15

Retail Therapy

It's surprising how much buying a new
pair of sneaks, the latest micro-mini, or
some pretty silk pjs can do for the
sagging spirit. A little recreational
relief shopping can't mend a crushed heart,
but it can help heal it—at least temporarily.
It's been unscientifically proven.

So why not plan an afternoon outing with
a friend or two to the local shopping district or mall?
You can dish dirt about your ex-crush in the dressing
room and swap single-girl stories in the shoe depart-
ment. It's easier on your teeth than chocolate, and it's
certainly better than moping around at home, alone and
miserable. Just don't go crazy and blow your whole
wad. Once you're feeling back to your old lucky
self again, you might want to put that money to
better use ...

Over and Out:
15 He's-So-Last-Season Songs

1. "Me, Myself, and I"—Beyoncé
2. "Since You've Been Gone"—Kelly Clarkson
3. "Everyday I Love You Less and Less"—Kaiser Chiefs
4. "Caught Out There"—Kelis
5. "My Happy Ending"—Avril Lavigne
6. "I Can See Clearly Now"—Everlife (or Jimmy Cliff)
7. "Stumble and Fall"—Razorlight
8. "Don't Bother"—Shakira
9. "The Comeback"—Shout Out Louds
10. "L.O.V.E."—Ashlee Simpson
11. "Hollaback Girl"—Gwen Stefani
12. "Cry Me a River"—Justin Timberlake
13. "Me Voy"—Julieta Venegas
14. "Kiss Off"—Violent Femmes
15. "Little Acorns"—The White Stripes

Crush Funeral

Dear friend, we are gathered here today to bury the past— and your crush (metaphorically speaking). Whether your love never actually got off the ground or it blossomed into a relationship that quickly crashed and burned, it's over now. And this is sad.

The heart-pounding emails, the notes, the doodles, the mementos, the IMs—all those reminders deserve to be saluted (briefly) and then buried, deleted, erased, filed, or simply stored on a key drive somewhere. You need to put them someplace they can live out of sight until you're ready to look back. When, you ask? Maybe when the thought of him no longer makes you feel like you're trapped on the teacup ride spinning round in circles or wearing your skin inside out.

Having a crush funeral doesn't have to be a big production. It takes just a few minutes (OK, maybe hours, if it was a big one), and it can be a soothing exercise—a final way to say *sayonara* to something you loved and lost. In a way, it's a happy occasion. Think of it as a funeral where no one actually died.

GETTING OVER IT

❝[Hitting a] punching bag always helps. You tape the person's pic up there and then go for it.❞ —13

New Mindset Mantras

A mantra is something you say over and over to remind yourself of a truth that you've forgotten. It's kind of like a spoken meditation. Get comfy, close your eyes, take some deep breaths, and repeat your chosen mantra. Say it aloud (or in your head) at least 10 times, or more if necessary, and you'll be fluttering about like a social butterfly before you know it. It's best to make up your own, but in case you get stuck here are a few suggestions to get you thinking.